Fiddles on the Bandstand

Fun Duets for Violin and Cello

Book One

by Myanna Harvey

Cover Image:
Camille Silvy (French, 1834 -1910)
M. Jullien's Orchestra, 1864, Albumen silver print
11 × 16.7 cm (4 5/16 × 6 9/16 in.), 84.XO.607.3
The J. Paul Getty Museum, Los Angeles

CHP378

©2020 by C. Harvey Publications All Rights Reserved.

www.charveypublications.com - print books
www.learnstrings.com - PDF downloadable books
www.harveystringarrangements.com - chamber music

Fiddles on the Bandstand: Fun Duets for Violin and Cello Book One

all duets arranged by Myanna Harvey

Table of Contents

	Title	Page
1.	The Entertainer (Scott Joplin)	2
2.	Take Me Out to the Ball Game (Albert Von Tilzer)	4
3.	Yankee Doodle (Traditional)	6
4.	The Stars and Stripes Forever (John Philip Sousa)	8
5.	El Jarabe Tapatio; *Mexican Hat Dance* (Traditional)	12
6.	Overture to *William Tell* (Gioachino Rossini)	14
7.	America the Beautiful (Samuel A. Ward)	16
8.	I'm a Yankee Doodle Dandy (George M. Cohan)	18
9.	Jeanie with the Light Brown Hair (Stephen Foster)	20
10.	My Country, 'Tis of Thee (Traditional)	21
11.	Drill, Ye Tarriers, Drill (Charles Connolly)	22
12.	Maple Leaf Rag (Scott Joplin)	24
13.	Over There (George M. Cohan)	26
14.	Simple Gifts (Traditional)	28
15.	The Washington Post March (John Philip Sousa)	30
16.	Let Me Call You Sweetheart (Leo Friedman)	34
17.	The Star Spangled Banner (John Stafford Smith)	35
18.	Funiculì, Funiculà (Luigi Denza)	36
19.	You're a Grand Old Flag (George M. Cohan)	38
20.	Summer, from *The Four Seasons* (Antonio Vivaldi)	40
21.	Armed Forces Medley (Various)	42
22.	Pomp and Circumstance March No. 1 (Edward Elgar)	45
23.	Overture to *The Barber of Seville* (Gioachino Rossini)	49

Fiddles on the Bandstand
Fun Duets for Violin and Cello, Book One

The Entertainer

S. Joplin, arr. M. Harvey

©2020 C. Harvey Publications All Rights Reserved.

Fiddles on the Bandstand for Violin and Cello, Book One

©2020 C. Harvey Publications All Rights Reserved.

Take Me Out to the Ball Game

A. Von Tilzer, arr. M. Harvey

Fiddles on the Bandstand for Violin and Cello, Book One

©2020 C. Harvey Publications All Rights Reserved.

Yankee Doodle

Trad., arr. M. Harvey

Fiddles on the Bandstand for Violin and Cello, Book One

The Stars and Stripes Forever

J. Sousa, arr. M. Harvey

Fiddles on the Bandstand for Violin and Cello, Book One

Fiddles on the Bandstand for Violin and Cello, Book One

Fiddles on the Bandstand for Violin and Cello, Book One

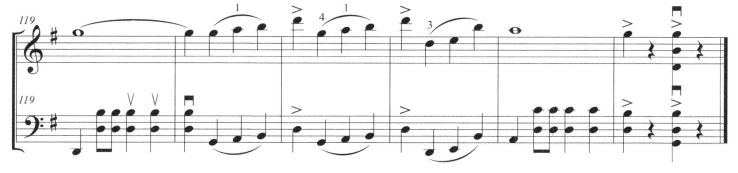

©2020 C. Harvey Publications All Rights Reserved.

El Jarabe Tapatio; *Mexican Hat Dance*

Trad., arr. M. Harvey

Overture to William Tell

G. Rossini, arr. M. Harvey

America the Beautiful

S. Ward, arr. M. Harvey

Fiddles on the Bandstand for Violin and Cello, Book One

I'm a Yankee Doodle Dandy

G. Cohan, arr. M. Harvey

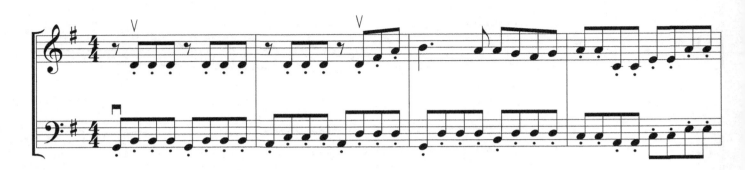

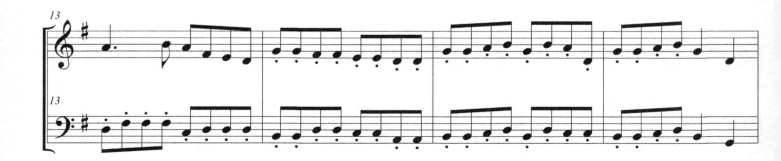

Fiddles on the Bandstand for Violin and Cello, Book One

Jeanie With the Light Brown Hair

S. Foster, arr. M. Harvey

molto rit.

molto rit.

My Country, 'Tis of Thee

Trad., arr. M. Harvey

Drill, Ye Tarriers, Drill

C. Connolly, arr. M. Harvey

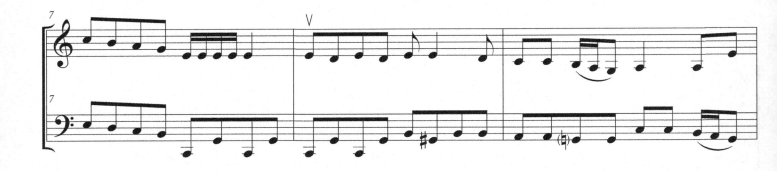

Fiddles on the Bandstand for Violin and Cello, Book One

Maple Leaf Rag

S. Joplin, arr. M. Harvey

Fiddles on the Bandstand for Violin and Cello, Book One

Over There

G. Cohan, arr. M. Harvey

Fiddles on the Bandstand for Violin and Cello, Book One

©2020 C. Harvey Publications All Rights Reserved.

Simple Gifts

Trad., arr. M. Harvey

Fiddles on the Bandstand for Violin and Cello, Book One

29

©2020 C. Harvey Publications All Rights Reserved.

The Washington Post March

J. Sousa, arr. M. Harvey

Fiddles on the Bandstand for Violin and Cello, Book One

32 Fiddles on the Bandstand for Violin and Cello, Book One

©2020 C. Harvey Publications All Rights Reserved.

Fiddles on the Bandstand for Violin and Cello, Book One

Let Me Call You Sweetheart

L. Friedman, arr. M. Harvey

The Star Spangled Banner

J. Smith, arr. M. Harvey

©2020 C. Harvey Publications All Rights Reserved.

Funiculì, Funiculà

L. Denza, arr. M. Harvey

Fiddles on the Bandstand for Violin and Cello, Book One

You're a Grand Old Flag

G. Cohan, arr. M. Harvey

Fiddles on the Bandstand for Violin and Cello, Book One

Summer, from *The Four Seasons*

A. Vivaldi, arr. M. Harvey

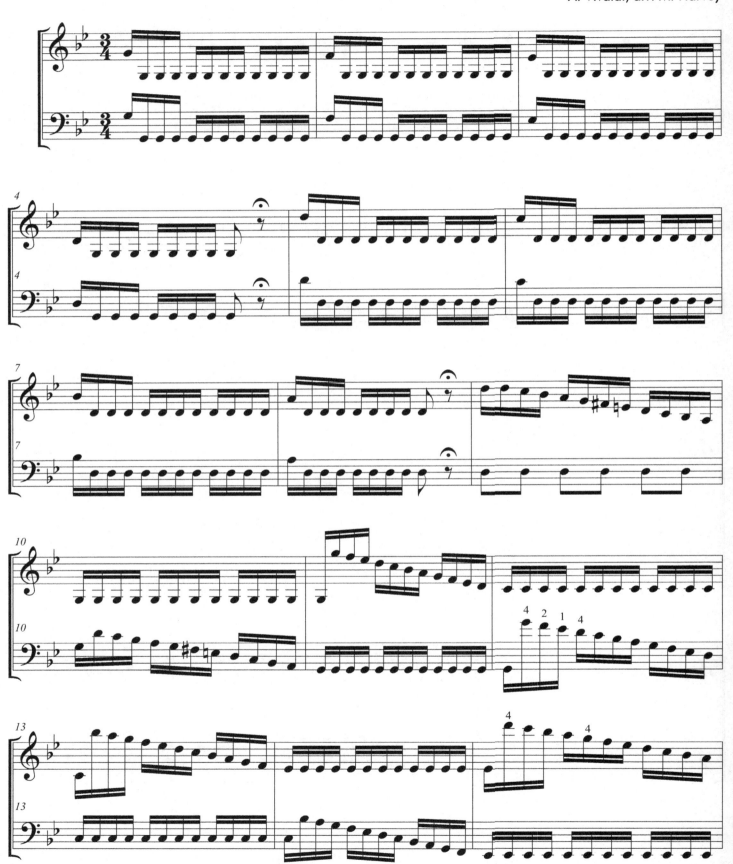

Fiddles on the Bandstand for Violin and Cello, Book One 41

©2020 C. Harvey Publications All Rights Reserved.

Armed Forces Medley

The Army Goes Rolling Along *(The Caissons Song)* — J. Sousa, arr. M. Harvey

Marine's Hymn — J. Offenbach, arr. M. Harvey

Fiddles on the Bandstand for Violin and Cello, Book One

Anchors Aweigh

C. Zimmermann, arr. M. Harvey

©2020 C. Harvey Publications All Rights Reserved.

This Page Left Blank for Page Turns

Pomp and Circumstance March No. 1

E. Elgar, arr. M. Harvey

Fiddles on the Bandstand for Violin and Cello, Book One

©2020 C. Harvey Publications All Rights Reserved.

This Page Left Blank for Page Turns

Fiddles on the Bandstand for Violin and Cello, Book One

Overture to *The Barber of Seville*

G. Rossini, arr. M. Harvey

Fiddles on the Bandstand for Violin and Cello, Book One

Available from www.charveypublications.com
Dancing Into Bethlehem: Compatible Christmas Duets for Strings

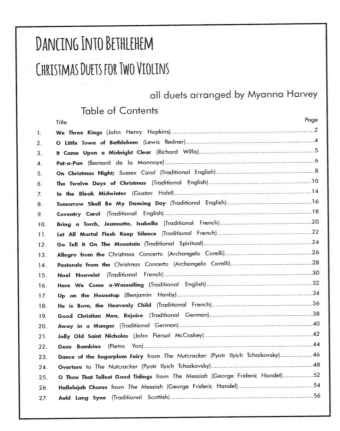

CHP360

CHP361

CHP362

Made in the USA
Monee, IL
18 December 2021